STRUM & SING

Ed Sheeran

Cover photo © London Entertainment / Alamy Stock Photo

ISBN 978-1-4950-4850-0

HAL•LEONARD®
CORPORATION

7777 W. BLUEMOUND RD. P.O. BOX 13819 MILWAUKEE, WI 53213

Visit Hal Leonard Online at
www.halleonard.com

The A Team

Words and Music by
Ed Sheeran

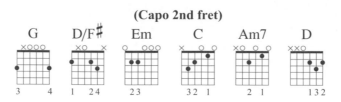

(Capo 2nd fret)

G   D/F♯   Em   C   Am7   D

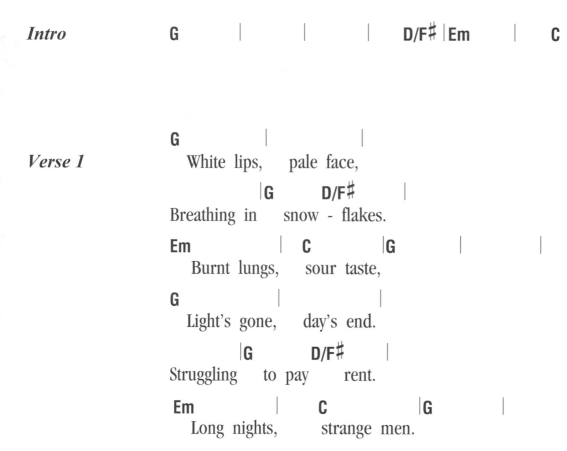

Intro   G | | | D/F♯ |Em | C |G | ||

Verse 1   G | | |
White lips,   pale face,

|G   D/F♯ |
Breathing in   snow - flakes.

Em |C |G | |
Burnt lungs,   sour taste,

G | |
Light's gone,   day's end.

|G   D/F♯ |
Struggling   to pay   rent.

Em |C |G |
Long nights,   strange men.

Pre-Chorus

‖**Am7**
And they   say

|**Am7** |**C** |
She's in the Class A   Team,

C |**G** |
Stuck in her day - dream.

G |**D**
Been this way since eighteen.

|**D** |**Am7** |
But lately her face seems

Am7 |**C** |
Slowly sinking, wast - ing,

C |**G**
Crumbling like pas - tries.

|**G**
And they   scream:

|**D** |
The worst   things in life come free to us.

Chorus 1

```
                    ‖Em             |C                      |
        'Cause we're just under the upper hand
        G                      |                    |
            And go mad for a couple grams.
        Em                          |C      |G       |
            And she don't want to go   outside   tonight.
                    |Em                 |C          |
        And in a pipe she flies to the motherland
        G                      |                 |
            Or sells love to an - other man.
        Em          |C          |G
            It's too cold    outside
                |D          |Em      |C         |G
        For an - gels to fly,
            |G              |Em       |C       |G      |         ‖
        An - gels to fly.
```

Verse 2

```
        G                  |            |
            Ripped gloves,    raincoat,
                        |G      D/F♯       |
        Tried to swim    stay    afloat.
        Em          |  C        |G       |            |
            Dry house,   wet  clothes,
        G              |              |
            Loose change,    bank notes.
                    |G      D/F♯      |
        Weary-eyed,    dry    throat.
        Em        |  C       |G        |
            Call girl,    no phone.
```

Repeat Pre-Chorus

6

Chorus 2

‖**Em** |**C** |
'Cause we're just under the upper hand

G | |
And go mad for a couple grams.

Em |**C** |**G** |
And she don't want to go   outside   tonight.

|**Em** |**C** |
And in a pipe she flies to the motherland

G | |
Or sells love to an - other man.

Em |**C** |**G**
It's too cold   outside

|**D** |**Am7**
For an - gels to fly.

|**Am7** |**C** |
That angel will die,

C |**Em** |
Covered in white,

Em |**G** |
Closed eye and hoping for a better life.

|**Am7** | |**C** |
This   time,   we'll fade out to - night,

C |**Em** |**C** |**G** | |
Straight down the line.

Em |**C** |**G** |

Repeat Pre-Chorus

Chorus 3

‖**Em** |**C** |
And we're all under the upper hand,

G | |
Go mad for a couple grams.

Em |**C** |**G** |
And we don't want to go outside tonight.

|**Em** |**C** |
And in the pipe we fly to the motherland

G | |
Or sell love to an - other man.

Em |**C** |**G**
It's too cold outside

|**D** |**Em** |**C** |**G**
For an - gels to fly,

|**G** |**Em** |**C** |**G** |
An - gels to fly,

|**Em** |**C** |**G**
To fly, fly,

|**G** |**Em** |**C** |**G** |
For angels to fly, to fly, to fly.

D |**G** ‖
Angels to die.

Bloodstream

Words and Music by Ed Sheeran,
Amir Izadkhah, Kesi Dryden, Piers Aggett,
John McDaid and Gary Lightbody

DADGAD tuning:
(low to high) D-A-D-G-A-D

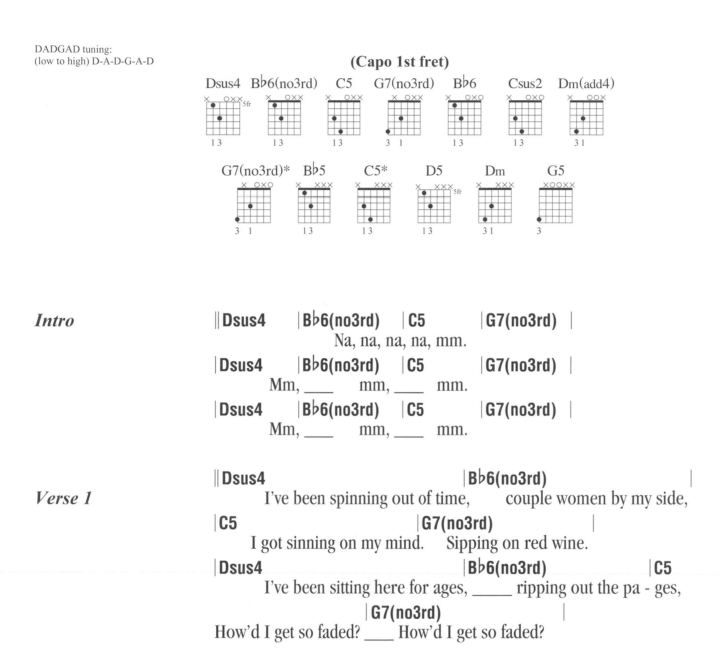

(Capo 1st fret)

Intro

‖Dsus4 |B♭6(no3rd) |C5 |G7(no3rd) |
            Na, na, na, na, mm.

|Dsus4 |B♭6(no3rd) |C5 |G7(no3rd) |
     Mm, ___   mm, ___ mm.

|Dsus4 |B♭6(no3rd) |C5 |G7(no3rd) |
     Mm, ___   mm, ___ mm.

Verse 1

‖Dsus4 |B♭6(no3rd) |
          I've been spinning out of time,   couple women by my side,

|C5 |G7(no3rd) |
     I got sinning on my mind.   Sipping on red wine.

|Dsus4 |B♭6(no3rd) |C5
     I've been sitting here for ages, ____ ripping out the pa - ges,

          |G7(no3rd) |
How'd I get so faded? ____ How'd I get so faded?

Pre-Chorus 1

```
‖Dsus4                          |B♭6(no3rd)
  Oh, no, no, don't leave me lone - ly now
              |C5                  |G7(no3rd)  |
If you loved ___ me how'd you never learn?
|Dsus4                          |B♭6(no3rd)
 Ooh, colored crimson in my eyes.
                              |C5        |G7(no3rd)  |
One or two could free my mind.
|B♭6       Csus2     |Dm(add4)
   This is how it ends,    I feel the chemicals
      |B♭6       Csus2              |G7(no3rd)*  |
Burn ___ in my       bloodstream.
|B♭6           Csus2     |Dm(add4)
   Fading out ___ again,       I feel the chemicals
      |B♭6       Csus2                  |
Burn ___ in my       bloodstream.
```

Chorus 1

```
|G7(no3rd)                       ‖Dsus4      |B♭6(no3rd)
   So tell me when it kicks in, _____ mm,
      |C5       |G7(no3rd)
Mm, ___ mm.
                              |Dsus4
Well, tell me when it kicks in,
   |B♭6(no3rd) |C5        |G7(no3rd)  |
Mm, ___    mm, ___ mm.
```

Verse 2

```
‖Dsus4                          |
   I've been looking for a lover,
|B♭6(no3rd)                       |
   Thought I'd find her in a bottle,
|C5                       |G7(no3rd)                |
   God make me another one.    I'll be feeling this tomorrow.
|Dsus4                          |B♭6(no3rd)
   Lord, forgive me for the things I've ___ done,
                          |C5
I was never meant to hurt no one,
                  |G7(no3rd)              |
And I saw scars upon a ___ broken hearted lover.
```

Pre-Chorus 2   *Repeat Pre-Chorus 1*

Chorus 2

| G7(no3rd)   ‖Dsus4 |B♭6(no3rd)
     So tell me when it kicks in, _____ mm,

|C5 |G7(no3rd)
Mm, ___ mm.

                           |D5
Well, tell me when it kicks in,

 |B♭6(no3rd) |C5 |G7(no3rd)
Mm, ___ mm, ___ mm.

                        |

Well, tell me when it kicks in.

Outro

‖B♭6   Csus2 |Dm(add4) |
     All the voices in my mind calling out across the

‖: B♭6   Csus2 |Dm(add4)   :‖ *Play 5 times*
   Line. All the voices in my mind calling out across the

|B♭6 Csus2 |
 Line. So tell me when it kicks in.

|Dm(add4) |B♭6   Csus2 |
   And I saw scars ___ upon her, tell me when it kicks in.

‖: Dm(add4) |B♭6   Csus2 |
   Broken heart - ed, so tell me when it kicks in.

|Dm(add4) |B♭6   Csus2   :‖ *Play 3 times*
   And I saw scars ___ upon her, tell me when it kicks in.

‖: Dm(add4) |B♭6(no3rd) C5* |
   Broken heart - ed, so tell me when it kicks in.

|Dsus4 |B♭6(no3rd)   C5*   :‖
   And I saw scars ___ upon her, tell me when it kicks in.

|Dsus4   Dm |G5   ‖
     Broken heart - ed.

All of the Stars

from the Motion Picture Soundtrack THE FAULT IN OUR STARS

Words and Music by
Ed Sheeran and John McDaid

Tune down 1/2 step:
(low to high) Eb - Ab - Db - Gb - Bb - Eb

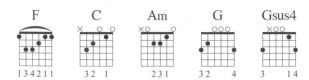

Verse 1

‖F   C |Am G F |
It's just another night   and I'm star - ing at the moon.

|C |G |
I saw a shooting star and thought of you.

|F   C |Am Gsus4   F |
I sing a lullaby   by the wa - ter   -   side and knew

|C |Gsus4 |
If you were here, I'd sing to you.

|F   C |Am G F |
You're on the other side   as the sky - line splits in two,

|C |Gsus4 G |
Miles away from see - ing you.

|F   C |Am Gsus4   F |
But I can see the stars   from A - mer - ica,

|C |G |
I wonder, do you see them too?

Chorus 1

                        ‖C |
So open your eyes and see

| |G |
The way our ho - rizons meet.

| |Am |
And all of the lights will leave

| |F |
Into the night with me.

| |C |
And I know these ___ scars will bleed

| |Gsus4 |
But both of our hearts believe

| |Am   F |C G |C |
All of these ___ stars will ___ guide ___ us ___ home.

Verse 2

```
 ‖F                       C      |Am   G   F      |
  I can hear your heart    on the ra  - di - o beat;
 |C                                   |G           |
  They're playing "Chasing Cars" and I thought of us.
 |F               C      |Am   Gsus4   F      |
  Back to the time   you were ly - ing      next to me,
 |C                      |Gsus4     G |
  I looked across and fell in love.
 |F                       C           |Am   G   F       |
  So I took your hand    back through lamp - lit  streets and dew,
 |C                      |Gsus4   G       |
  Ev'rything led back to you.
 |F                        C   |Am   Gsus4   F      |
  So can you see the stars ___ over Am - ster  -  dam?
 |C                               |G           |
  Hear the song our heart is beat - ing to.
```

Chorus 2

```
 N.C.           ‖C           |
  So open your eyes and see
 |                     |G           |
  The way our ho - rizons meet.
 |                 |Am          |
  And all of the lights will leave
 |          |F               |
  Into the night with me.
 |                  |C              |
  And I know these ___ scars will bleed
 |            |Gsus4        |
  But both of our hearts believe
 |              |Am          F    |C    G    |
  All of these ___ stars will ___ guide ___ us ___ home.
```

Bridge

```
        ‖F     |G
  And oh.
        |Am    |C
  And oh.
        |F     |G    |C    |        |
  And oh.
```

Outro

```
 ‖F                   C      |Am   Gsus4   F   ‖
  I can see the stars   from A - mer - i  -  ca.
```

Don't

Words and Music by Ed Sheeran, Dawn Robinson, Benjamin Levin,
Raphael Saadiq, Ali Jones-Muhammad and Conesha Owens

Tune down 1/2 step:
(low to high) Eb - Ab - Db - Gb - Bb - Eb

F#m7 C#m7 D E

Intro

| N.C. |

(Ah, la, 'n, la, la.

| F#m7 C#m7 | D E |

| F#m7 C#m7 | D E |

Ah, la, 'n, la, la.)

Verse 1

|F#m7   C#m7
 I met this girl late last year,

|D   E
She said, "Don't you worry if I disappear."

|F#m7   C#m7
I told her, "I'm not really looking for a - nother mistake,"

|D   E
I called an old friend, thinking that the trouble would wait.

|F#m7   C#m7
But then I jump right in a week later returned,

|D   E
I reckon she was only looking for a lover to burn.

|F#m7   C#m7
But I gave her my time for two or three nights,

|D   E
Then I put it on pause until the moment was right.

|F#m7 C#m7 |D   E
I went a - way, four months un - til our paths crossed a - gain.

|F#m7   C#m7
She told me, "I was never looking for a friend,

|D   E
Maybe you could swing by my room around ten.

|F#m7   C#m7
Baby, bring the lemon and a bottle of gin,

|D   E
We'll be in between the sheets 'til the late a. - m."

|F#m7   C#m7
Baby, if you wanted me then you should've just said.

|
She's singing:

Chorus 1

```
|D                E           |F#m7
(Ah, la, 'n,     la,          la)
            Don't fuck with my love.
      C#m7   |D        E     |F#m7
That heart is so cold, all over my home.
            C#m7                |
I don't wanna know that, babe.
|D                E           |F#m7
(Ah, la, 'n,     la,          la.
            Don't fuck with my love.
  C#m7       |D         E          |F#m7
I told her, she knows, take aim and re - load.
            C#m7                |
I don't wanna know that, babe.
|D        E
(Ah, la, 'n, la, la.)
```

Verse 2

```
              |F#m7              C#m7
And for a couple weeks I only wan - na see her,
                     |D                   E
We drink away the days with a take-away pizza.
       |F#m7                       C#m7
Before, a text message was the only way to reach her,
                     |D                         E
Now she's staying at my place and loves the way I treat her.
          |F#m7             C#m7
Singing out Ar - etha, all over the track like a feature,
        |D                          E             |
And never wants to sleep, I guess that I don't want to either.
|F#m7                        C#m7              |
   But me and her, we make mon - ey the same way,
|D                      E                |
  Four cities, two planes, ____ the same day.
|F#m7                        C#m7
   And those shows have never been what it's about,
          |D                      E
But may - be we'll go together and just figure it out.
        |F#m7                     C#m7
I'd rather put on a film with you and sit on the couch
                   |D                    E
But we should get on a plane or we'll be missing it now.
          |F#m7                   C#m7
Wish I'd have written it down the way that things played out,
                 |D                     E
When she was kissing him, how I was con - fused about.
              |F#m7               C#m7            |
Now she should figure it out while I'm sat here singing:
```

Chorus 2   *Repeat Chorus 1*

Verse 3

```
|F#m7                        C#m7          |
(Knock, knock, knock) on my hotel door,
|D                   E
 I don't even know if she knows what for.
       |F#m7                  C#m7          |
She was crying on my shoulder, I already told ya,
|D                    E          |
 Trust and respect is what we do this for.
|F#m7             C#m7
 I never intended to be next,
        |D                    E           |
But you didn't need to take him to bed, that's all.
|F#m7                C#m7
 And I never saw him as a threat
             |D                       E          |
Until you disappeared with him to have sex, of course.
|F#m7                 C#m7
   It's not like we were both on tour,
             |D                  E
We were staying on the same fucking hotel floor.
       |F#m7                         C#m7
And I wasn't looking for a promise or commitment
             |D               E            |
But it was never just fun, and I thought you were diff'rent.
|F#m7                   C#m7
 This is not the way you rea - lize what you wanted,
          |D             E
It's a bit too much, too late if I'm honest.
    |F#m7              C#m7           |
And all this time, God knows I'm singing:
```

Chorus 3

```
|: D            E         |F#m7
(Ah, la, 'n,    la,       la.)
         Don't fuck with my love.
      C#m7       |D      E    |F#m7
That heart is so cold, all over my home.
          C#m7                |
I don't wanna know that, babe.
|D          E              |F#m7
(Ah, la, 'n,    la,       la.)
         Don't fuck with my love.
   C#m7         |D        E          |F#m7
I told her, she knows, take aim and re - load.
           C#m7            :|| N.C.              ||
I don't wanna know that, babe. (Ah, la, 'n, la, la.)
```

Drunk

Words and Music by
Ed Sheeran and Jake Gosling

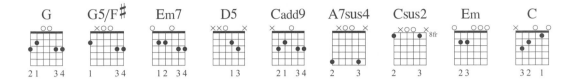

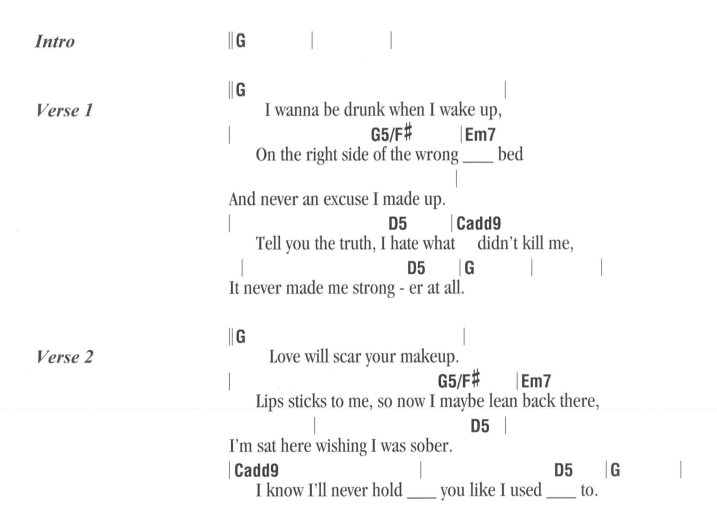

Intro ‖G | |

Verse 1

‖G |
I wanna be drunk when I wake up,

                                         G5/F♯ |Em7
On the right side of the wrong ___ bed

                                        |
And never an excuse I made up.

                            D5 |Cadd9
Tell you the truth, I hate what   didn't kill me,

                            D5 |G | |
It never made me strong - er at all.

Verse 2

‖G |
Love will scar your makeup.

                                 G5/F♯ |Em7
Lips sticks to me, so now I maybe lean back there,

                | D5 |
I'm sat here wishing I was sober.

|Cadd9 | D5 |G |
I know I'll never hold ___ you like I used ___ to.

Pre-Chorus 1

```
|          ‖Em7                         D5              |
         But a house gets cold when you cut the heating
|G                  Cadd9          |
 Without you to hold, I'll be freezing.
|Em7             D5              |
  Can't rely on my heart to beat in,
|G                      Cadd9        |
 'Cause you take parts of it ev'ry evening.
|Em7                       D5             |
 Take words out of my mouth just from breathing.
|G                          Cadd9          |G
 Replace with phrases like "When you leaving me?"
                A7sus4        |Csus2
 Should I? ___ Should I?
```

Chorus 1

```
            ‖Em7          |G
         Maybe I'll get drunk again.
         |Em            |G
 I'll be ___ drunk again,
         |Em              |G          |C   |D5    |
 I'll be ___ drunk again ___ to feel a little love.
```

Verse 3

```
‖G                                    |
         I wanna hold your heart in both hands
|                                G5/F♯      |
 Not watch it fizzle at the bottom of a Coke can.
|Em7                          |
         And I got no plans for the weekend,
|                                    D5         |
         So should we speak then? Keep it between ___ friends,
|Cadd9                          |
         Though I know you'll never love ___ me
                 D5    |G       |      |
 Like you used ___ to.
```

Verse 4

```
  ‖G                                        |
          There may be other people like us
  |                                   G5/F♯   |
       Who see the flicker of the clipper when they light up.
  |Em7                    |            D5   |Cadd9
   Flames just create us, but burns don't heal like be - fore.
            |                    D5  |G      |
   And you don't hold me anymore.
```

Pre-Chorus 2

```
  |       ‖Em7            D5                      |
           On cold days cold plays out like the band's name.
  |G                       Cadd9                  |
       I know I can't heal things ___ with a handshake.
  |Em7                   D5              |
       You know I can change, as I began saying,
  |G                       Cadd9           |
       You caught me wide open like landscape.
  |Em7                 D5                   |
       Open bottles of beer, but never champagne,
  |G                         Cadd9               |
   To applaud you with the sound ___ that my hands make.
  |G          A7sus4      |Csus2
   Should I? ___ Should I?
```

Chorus 2   *Repeat Chorus 1*

Bridge

```
  ‖Em7        Cadd9  |G                    |
       All by my - self, _____ I'm here again
  |Em7        Cadd9  |G                        |
       All by my - self, _____ you know I'll never change.
  |Em7        Cadd9  |G      |
       All by my - self,
  |Cadd9        D5     |Em
       All by my - self.
```

Outro-Chorus

```
            |Em             |G
  I'm just ___ drunk again.
            |Em             |G
  I'll be ___ drunk again.
            |Em          |G            |C     |D5     ‖
  I'll be   drunk again ___ to feel a little love.
```

Give Me Love

Words and Music by Ed Sheeran,
Chris Leonard and Jake Gosling

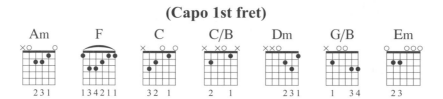

Intro   ‖: Am |F |C | C/B :‖ *Play 4 times*

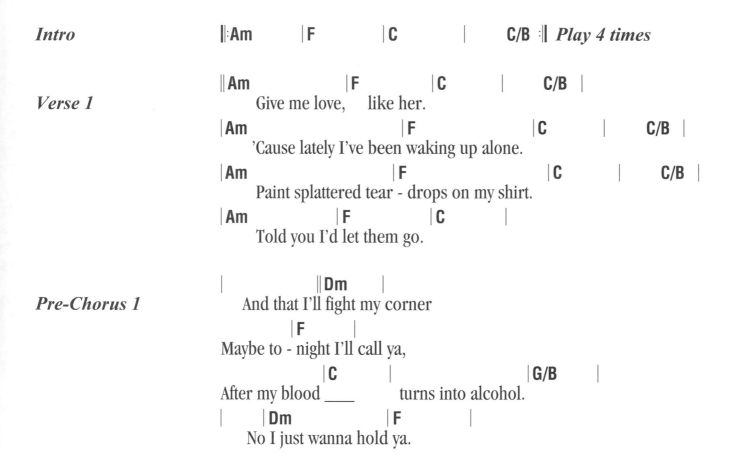

Verse 1
‖Am |F |C | C/B |
Give me love,   like her.
|Am |F |C | C/B |
'Cause lately I've been waking up alone.
|Am |F |C | C/B |
Paint splattered tear - drops on my shirt.
|Am |F |C |
Told you I'd let them go.

Pre-Chorus 1
| ‖Dm |
And that I'll fight my corner
|F |
Maybe to - night I'll call ya,
|C | |G/B |
After my blood ___ turns into alcohol.
| |Dm |F |
No I just wanna hold ya.

Chorus 1

```
||C            Dm   |F                        |
   Give a little time to me, or burn this out.
|            Dm   |F                           |
   We'll play hide and seek to turn this around.
|C       Dm       |F                           |
   All I want is the taste that your lips allow.
|Am      G/B      |F                           |
   My my,    my my, ___ oh, give me love.
||: Am        F       |C                        |
   My my,    my my, ___ oh, give me love.
|Am          F       |C                      :||
   My my,    my my, ___ oh, give me love.
```

Verse 2

```
|Am            |F              |C      |    C/B |
   Give me love like never before.
|Am                  |F        |C      |    C/B |
   'Cause lately I've been craving more.
|Am                       |F       |C      |    C/B |
   And it's been a while, but I still feel the same.
|Am              |F       |C          |
   Maybe I should let you go.
```

Pre-Chorus 2

```
|              ||Dm     |
   You know I'll fight my corner
          |F        |
And that to - night I'll call ya,
             |C     |                    |G/B      |
After my blood ____   is drowning in alcohol.
|      |Dm        |F        |
   No, I just wanna hold ya.
```

Chorus 2

‖: C   **Dm** |F |C
Give a little time to me, or burn this out.

         Dm |F |
We'll play hide and seek to turn this around.

|C   **Dm** |F |
All I want is the taste that your lips allow.

|Am   **G/B** |F   :‖
My my,   my my, ___ oh, give me love.

‖: Am   **F** |C |
My my,   my my, ___ oh, give me love.

|Am   **F** |C   :‖
My my,   my my, ___ oh, give me love.

Bridge

‖: Am | **Em**   :‖ *Play 7 times*
(M, my, my, a, m, my, my a, m, my, my, a, gimme love, lover.)

|Am | **Em** |
Love me. Love me.

|Am | **Em** |
Love me.   Give me love.

|Am | **Em** |
Give me love.

|Am | **Em** |Am | **Em** |
Give me love.   Love me.   Give me love.

Outro-Chorus

‖: Am |F |
My, my, my, my, ___ oh, give me love.

|C | :‖ *Play 5 times*
My, my, my, my, ___ oh, give me love.

|Am |F |
My, my, my, my, ___ oh, give me love.

|C |**N.C.**   ‖
My, my, my, my, ____ oh, give me love.

I See Fire

Words and Music by
Ed Sheeran

(Capo 6th fret)

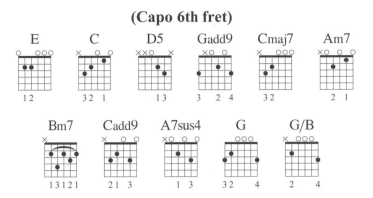

Intro

‖**N.C.(Em)** | | |
   Oh, misty eye of the mountain below,

| | |
Keep careful watch of my brothers' souls.

| | |
And should the sky be filled with fire and smoke,

| | |
Keep watching over Durin's Sons.
|**Em**   **C** |**D5**   **Em** | **C** |

Verse 1

|**D5**   **Em** ‖**Em**   **Gadd9**
       If this is to end in fire,
       |**D5**   **Cmaj7**
Then we should all burn ___ together,
    |**Em**   **Gadd9** |**D5**   **Am7**
Watch the flames climb high   into the night.
    |**Em**   **Gadd9** |**D5**   **Cmaj7**
Calling out, father, ___ oh, stand by and we will
    |**Am7**   **Bm7** |**Cmaj7** |**Em** **C** |
Watch the flames burn auburn on the mountain side.

Verse 2

```
|D5   Em                      ‖Em      Gadd9
        And if we should die to - night,
          |D5    Cmaj7
We should all die ___ together,
        |Em     Gadd9  |D5       Am7
Raise a glass of wine        for the last time.
        |Em      Gadd9  |D5       Cadd9
Calling out, father, ___ oh,  prepare as we will watch
     |Am7      Bm7         |Cmaj7
The flames burn auburn on the mountain side.
        |Am7  Bm7              |Cmaj7
Deso - lation  comes upon the sky.
```

Chorus 1

```
        ‖Em    Cadd9  |D5       Em
Now I see fire,            inside the mountain.
     |      Cadd9  |D5        Em
I see fire,         burning the trees.
        |      Cadd9  |D5       Em
And I see fire, _____   hollowing souls.
     |      Cadd9  |D5       Am7
I see fire, _____  blood in the breeze.
     |                         |
And I hope that you'll remember me.
```

Interlude

```
‖ Em    C   |D5    Em   |   C   |
```

Verse 3

```
|D5   Em                      ‖Em      Gadd9
        Oh, should my people fall,
          |D5       Cmaj7
Then surely I'll do the same.
        |Em     Gadd9      |D5      Cmaj7
Confined in mountain halls, we got too close to the flame.
        |Em      Gadd9  |D5       Cmaj7
Calling out, father, ___ oh,    hold fast and we will
     |Am7      Bm7         |Cmaj7
Watch the flames burn auburn on the mountain side.
        |Am7  Bm7              |Cmaj7
Deso - lation  comes upon the sky.
```

Chorus 2

```
          ‖Em    Cadd9  |D5        Em
Now I see fire,                inside the mountain.
     |      Cadd9  |D5        Em
I see fire,               burning the trees.
        |        Cadd9 |D5        Em
And I see fire _____   hollowing souls.
        |        Cadd9 |D5        Am7
I see fire, _____   blood in the breeze.
     |A7sus4                      |
And I hope that you remember me.
```

Bridge

```
     |              ‖Am7   Em          |G        D5
     And, if the night is burning, I will cover my eyes
       |Am7    Em          |G        D5
For if the dark re - turns, then my brothers will die.
       |Am7         Em         |G          D5
And as the sky is falling down, it crashed in - to this lonely town.
          |Am7
And with that shadow upon the ground,
  G/B     |C                      D5
I    hear my people screaming out.
```

Chorus 3

```
          ‖Em    Cadd9  |D5        Em
And I see fire,                inside the mountains.
     |      Cadd9  |D5        Em
I see fire,               burning the trees.
        |        Cadd9 |D5        Em
And I see fire, _____   hollowing souls.
     |      Cadd9 |D5        Em
I see fire, _____   blood in the breeze.
```

Outro

```
     ‖Em   Cadd9                      |D5   Em
I see fire,   oh, you know I saw a city burning.
     |        Cadd9                    |D5   Em
And I see fire,    feel the heat upon my skin.
     |        Cadd9        |D5  Em
And I see fire,   ooh, ooh, ooh, fire.
     |             Cadd9        |D5        Em   ‖
And I see fire burn auburn on the mountain side.
```

I'm a Mess

Words and Music by
Ed Sheeran

Tune down 1/2 step:
(low to high) E♭ - A♭ - D♭ - G♭ - B♭ - E♭

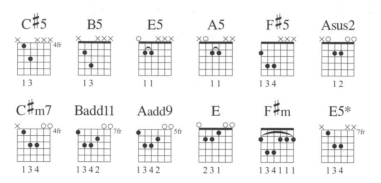

C#5   B5   E5   A5   F#5   Asus2

C#m7   Badd11   Aadd9   E   F#m   E5*

Verse 1

N.C.   ‖C#5 | |B5
   Oh, I'm a mess ___ right now,   inside out.

    | |E5
Search - ing for a sweet ___ surrender

 |A5 |E5 |
But this is not the end.

 | F#5 |C#5 | |B5 |
  I can't ___ work ___ it out,   how.

 | |E5 |
Going through the mo - tions,

|A5 |B5 |
 Going through us.

| |A5 | |E5
  And oh, I've known ___ it for the longest time

        |B5 |A5
And all of my hopes, ___ all of my own words,

    | |E5
Are all o - ver written on the signs

       |B5 |Asus2
But you're on my road, ___ walking me home,

     | |
Home, home, home, home.

Chorus 1

```
‖C#m7          |           |Badd11      |
     See the flames ___ inside my eyes,
|              |Aadd9   |                    |E      |      F#5|
     It burns so bright,   I wanna feel your love.           No.
|C#m7          |           |Badd11      |
     Easy, ba - by, maybe I'm a liar.
|              |Aadd9   |                 |E        |
     But for to - night     I wanna fall in love,
|              |F#m     |Aadd9        |
     And put your faith in my ___ stomach.
```

Verse 2

```
|              ‖C#5          |                |B5
     I messed up ___ this time,     late last night.
     |               |E5
Drink - ing to suppress ___ devotion
     |A5            |E5         |
With fingers intertwined.
|         F#5     |C#5      |            |B5
     I can't ___ shake ___ this feeling      now,
     |                  |E5         |
We're going through the mo  -  tions,
|A5              |B5        |
  Hoping you'd stop.
|        |A5           |
     And oh, I have on - ly caused you pain,
       |E5                |B5             |A5
I know ___ but all of my words ___ were always below
     |                 |E5                    |B5
Of all, ___ all the love you spoke ___ when you're on my road,
                 |Asus2          |            |
Walking me home, ___ home, home,    home, home.
```

Chorus 2   *Repeat Chorus 1*

Bridge

```
|          ‖C#5  E5*   B5    |          |A5  E5*   B5   |C#5    |
      And for    how   long ___ I love ___  my   lov  -  er.
|    E5*   B5    |          |A5   E5*   B5   |C#5             |
For how   long ___ I love ___  my   lov  - er, now, now?
|    E5*   B5    |          |A5   E5*   B5   |C#5             |
For how long, ___ long I love ___  my    lov  - er, now, now?
|    E5*   B5    |          |A5   E5*   B5   |C#5  N.C.       |
For how long, ___ long I love ___  my    lov  - er, now, now?
‖:C#m7   E5*   Badd11    |
   For   how   long, _____ long
      |Aadd9   E5*   Badd11  |C#m7            :‖ Play 4 times
I love _____ my    lov  -   er, now, now?
|C#5  E5*   B5    |          |A5  E5*   B5   |C#5             |
 For   how   long, ___ long I love ___  my   lov  - er, now, now?
|C#5  E5*   B5    |          |A5  E5*   B5   |C#5             |
 For   how   long, ___ long I love ___  my   lov  - er, now, now?
```

Outro

```
‖N.C.(C#5)   (E5)   (B5)  |N.C.      |(A5) (E5) (B5) |(C#5)                |
  For          how   long, ___ I love ___  my   lov  - er, now, now?
|(C#5)    (E5)   (B5)  |N.C.        |(A5) (B5) (C#5)  |               ‖
 For       how   long, ___ long I love ___  my    lov  -   er?
```

28

Kiss Me

Words and Music by Ed Sheeran,
Julie Frost, Justin Franks and Ernest Wilson

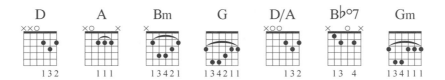

Intro ‖: D A Bm | A G | D | :‖

Verse 1
‖D A Bm |
Settle down with me,

| A G | D | |
Cover me up, cuddle me ___ in.

| A Bm |
Lie down with me,

| A G | D | |
And hold _____ me in your arms.

Pre-Chorus 1
‖G |A
And your heart's against my chest,

|
Your lips pressed to my neck.

|D |Bm |G
I'm falling for your eyes, ___ but they don't know me yet.

|A |
And with a feeling I'll forget, I'm in love now.

Chorus 1

```
 ‖D                    A    Bm  |
   Kiss me like you wanna be      loved,
     A    G |              D  |          |
   You wanna be loved, you wanna be ___ loved.
 |                    A    Bm  |
     This feels like falling in      love,
 A    G |          D    |        |
 Falling in love, falling in love.
```

Verse 2

```
 ‖D                  A    Bm  |
    Settle down with me,
 |                      A   G  |
    And I'll be your safe  -  ty,
                      D  |        |
 And you'll be my la - dy.
 |                  A   Bm        |
    I was made    to keep ___ your body warm,
 A      G  |                       D   |
    But I'm cold as the wind blows,   so hold me in your arms.
```

Pre-Chorus 2

```
        ‖G                              |A
 Oh, ___ no my heart's against your chest,
                                  |
 Your lips pressed to my neck.
 |D                       |Bm                        |G
    I'm falling for your eyes, ___ but they don't know me yet.
                               |A                       |
 And with this feeling I'll forget,   I'm in love now.
```

Chorus 2   *Repeat Chorus 1*

Guitar Solo   *Repeat Intro*

Bridge

‖ **D/A** |**B♭°7**

       Yeah, I've been feeling ev'ry - thing

                                    |**Bm**

From hate to love, from love to lust,

                  A |**G**

From lust to truth, I   guess that's how I know ___ you.

              |**Gm**

So, hold ___ you close, ___ to help you give it up.

Chorus 3

‖ **D**   **A**   **Bm** |

     So, kiss me like you wanna be   loved,

     A   **G** | **D** | |

You wanna be loved, you wanna be ___ loved.

| **A**   **Bm** |

     This feels like falling in   love,

A   **G** | **D** | |

Falling in love, falling in love.

Chorus 4   *Repeat Chorus 1*

Outro   *Repeat Intro and fade*

Lego House

Words and Music by Ed Sheeran,
Chris Leonard and Jake Gosling

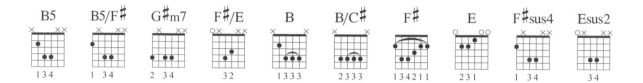

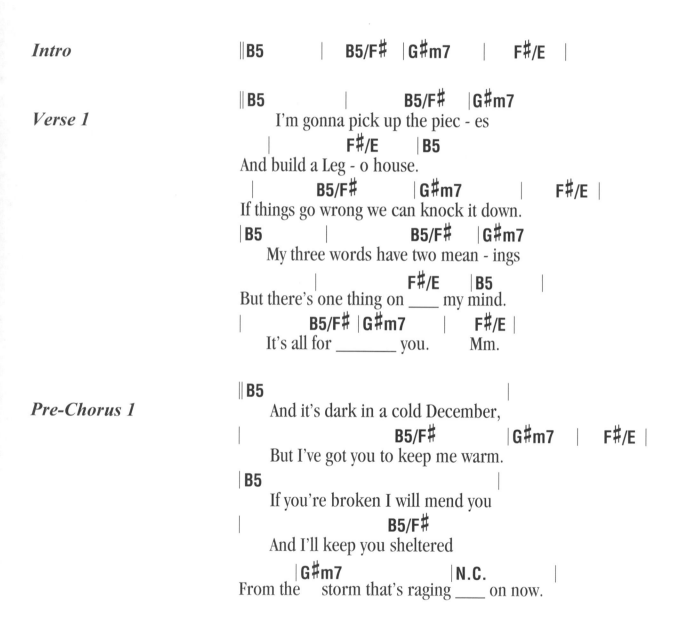

Intro ‖B5 | B5/F♯ |G♯m7 | F♯/E |

Verse 1

‖B5 | B5/F♯ |G♯m7
I'm gonna pick up the piec - es

| F♯/E |B5
And build a Leg - o house.

| B5/F♯ |G♯m7 | F♯/E |
If things go wrong we can knock it down.

|B5 | B5/F♯ |G♯m7
My three words have two mean - ings

| F♯/E |B5 |
But there's one thing on ____ my mind.

| B5/F♯ |G♯m7 | F♯/E |
It's all for _____ you.   Mm.

Pre-Chorus 1

‖B5 |
And it's dark in a cold December,

| B5/F♯ |G♯m7 | F♯/E |
But I've got you to keep me warm.

|B5 |
If you're broken I will mend you

| B5/F♯
And I'll keep you sheltered

|G♯m7 |N.C. |
From the   storm that's raging ____ on now.

Chorus 1

```
 ‖B                    |          B/C♯        |
     I'm out of touch,    I'm out of love,
 |G♯m7                 |          B           |F♯
     I'll pick you up    when you're getting down.
                |          G♯m7    |E
 And out of all these things I've done
                |          F♯           |
 I think I love you better now.
 |B                    |          B/C♯        |
     I'm out of sight,    I'm out of mind,
 |G♯m7                 |       B      |F♯
     I'll do it all for you in time.
                |          G♯m7    |E
 And out of all these things I've done,
                |          F♯           |
 I think I love you better now.
 |B            |             |G♯m7    |    F♯    |
                 Now.
```

Verse 2

```
 ‖B5                   |          B5/F♯   |G♯m7
     I'm gonna paint you by num - bers
          |          F♯/E         |
 And color you ____ in.
 |B5     |          B5/F♯      |G♯m7
     If things go right we can frame it
          |          F♯/E   |
 And put you on a wall.
 |B5            |          B5/F♯  |G♯m7
     And it's so hard to say _____ it
          |          F♯/E      |
 But I've been here be - fore.
 |B5            |             B5/F♯      |G♯m7
     Now, I'll sur - render up ____ my heart
          |          F♯/E   |
 And swap it for yours.
```

Chorus 2

```
            ‖B                 |        B/C♯        |
               I'm out of touch,    I'm out of love,
            |G♯m7              |              B/C♯        |F♯
               I'll pick you up     when you're getting down.
                      |            G♯m7    |E
            And out of all these things I've done
                      |        F♯         |
            I think I love you better now.
            |B                 |        B/C♯        |
               I'm out of sight,    I'm out of mind,
            |G♯m7          |      B    |F♯
               I'll do it all for you in time.
                      |            G♯m7    |E
            And out of all these things I've done,
                      |        F♯         |
            I think I love you better now.
```

Bridge

```
            ‖G♯m7  |F♯            |E         |
               Don't hold me down,
            |              |F♯                |
               I think the braces are breaking
            |          |E            |F♯      |
               And it's more than I can take.
```

Pre-Chorus 2

```
            ‖B5                              |
               And it's dark in a cold December,
            |                   B5/F♯      |G♯m7   |   F♯/E  |
               But I've got you to keep me warm.
            |B5                             |
               If you're broken I will mend you
            |                   B5/F♯
               And I'll keep you sheltered
               |G♯m7              |F♯/E        |
            From the    storm that's raging ___ on now.
```

Chorus 3

```
       ‖B                    |        B/C♯        |
          I'm out of touch,    I'm out of love,
      |G♯m7              |             B         |F♯
          I'll pick you up    when you're getting down.
                      |          G♯m7   |E
      And out of all these things I've done
                      |          F♯         |
      I think I love you better now.
      |B                    |        B/C♯        |
          I'm out of sight,    I'm out of mind,
      |G♯m7              |        B    |F♯
          I'll do it all for you in time.
                      |          G♯m7   |E
      And out of all these things I've done,
                      |          F♯         |
      I think I love you better now.
```

Outro-Chorus

```
       ‖B                    |        B/C♯        |
          I'm out of touch,    I'm out of love,
      |G♯m7              |             B/C♯        |F♯sus4
          I'll pick you up when you're getting down.
                      |          G♯m7   |Esus2
      And out of all these things I've done
                      |          F♯         |B        ‖
      I will love you better now.
```

One

Words and Music by
Ed Sheeran

DADGAD tuning, down 1 step:
(low to high) C-G-C-F-G-C

(Capo 2nd fret)

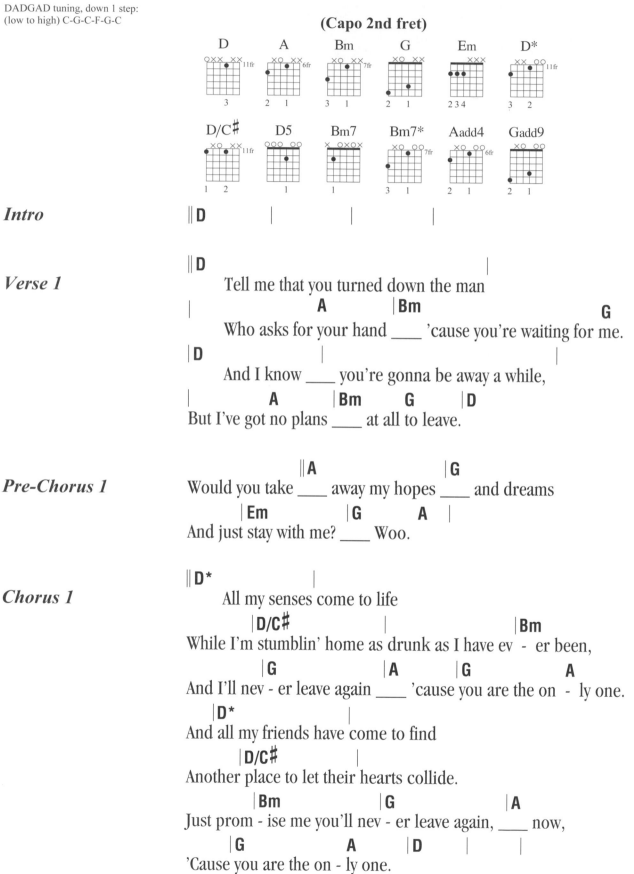

Intro

‖D

Verse 1

‖D
     Tell me that you turned down the man

           A   **Bm**   **G**
Who asks for your hand ____ 'cause you're waiting for me.

|D
And I know ____ you're gonna be away a while,

       A   **Bm**   **G** |D
But I've got no plans ____ at all to leave.

Pre-Chorus 1

          ‖**A**   **G**
Would you take ____ away my hopes ____ and dreams

       |**Em** |**G**   **A** |
And just stay with me? ____ Woo.

Chorus 1

‖**D***
    All my senses come to life

     |**D/C♯** |**Bm**
While I'm stumblin' home as drunk as I have ev - er been,

       |**G**   **A** |**G**   **A**
And I'll nev - er leave again ____ 'cause you are the on - ly one.

  |**D***
And all my friends have come to find

   |**D/C♯**
Another place to let their hearts collide.

     |**Bm** |**G** |**A**
Just prom - ise me you'll nev - er leave again, ____ now,

    |**G**   **A** |**D**
'Cause you are the on - ly one.

Verse 2

```
       ‖D                      |
              Take my hand and my    heart and soul.
      A     |Bm              G        |
I ___ will    only have these eyes for you.
|D                   |
       And you know ___ ev'rything changes,
       |                A   |Bm           G          |D
But ___ we'll be strangers ___ if ___ we see this ___ through.
```

Pre-Chorus 2

```
         ‖A                |G
We could stay within these walls ___ and play,
       |Bm           |G      A       |
Oh, just stay with me. ___ Oh, ___ Lord, now.
```

Chorus 2

```
       ‖D*            |
   All my senses come to life
            |D/C♯             |              |Bm
While I'm stumblin' home as drunk as I have ev - er been,
            |G          |A    |G        A
And I'll nev - er leave again ___ 'cause you are the on - ly one.
       |D*              |
And all my friends have come to find
         |D/C♯           |
Another place to let their hearts collide.
            |Bm              |G             |A
Just prom - ise me you'll al - ways be a friend, ___ now,
         |G       A       |
'Cause you are the on - ly one.
```

Bridge

```
‖G                        |D5                    |A
    Stumblin' off drunk, ___ gettin' myself lost.
              |   D5            Bm7        |G
I am so gone, ___ so tell me the way ___ home.
                      |D5                |A
I listen to sad songs ___ singin' about love
      |                    |
And where it goes wrong.
```

Interlude

```
‖ Bm     G   |D5          |Bm7   G   |
| D5          |Bm    G   |D5            |
| Bm7*  Aadd4 |Gadd9        |          |
```

Chorus 3

```
‖D*              |
  All my senses come to life
        |D/C♯            |                    |Bm
While I'm stumblin' home as drunk as I have ev - er been,
          |G          |A      |G          A
And I'll nev - er leave again ___ 'cause you are the on - ly one.
    |D*            |
And all my friends have come to find
       |D/C♯                  |
Another place to let their hearts collide.
         |Bm7*            |                |Aadd4
Just prom - ise me you'll al - ways be a friend,
        |Gadd9        A  |D5       ‖
'Cause you are the on - ly one.
```

Photograph

Words and Music by
Ed Sheeran and John McDaid

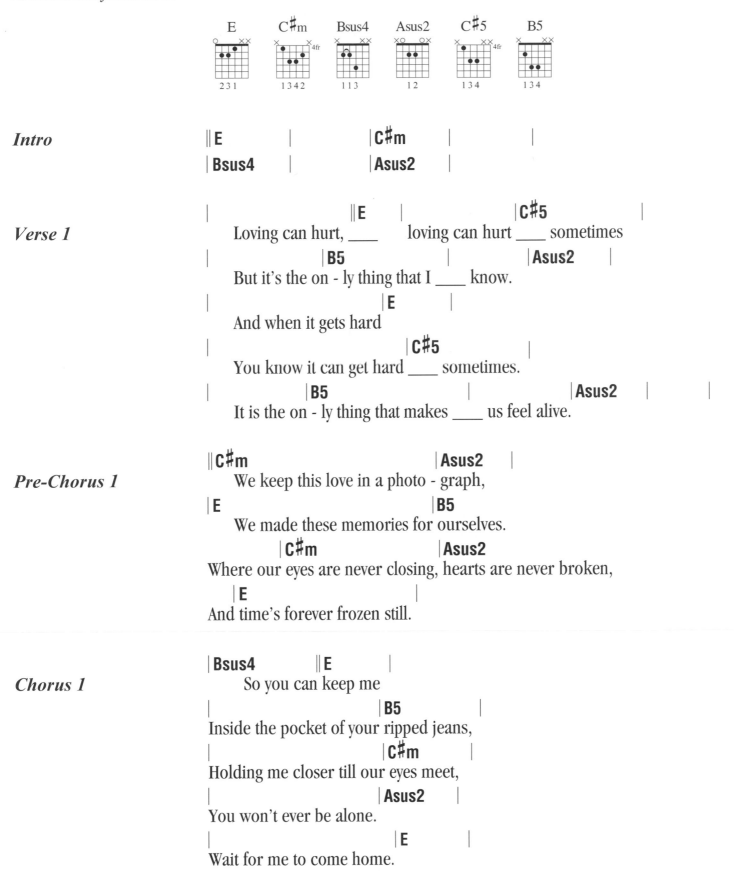

Intro

‖E | |C#m | |
|Bsus4 | |Asus2 |

Verse 1

| ‖E | |C#5 |
Loving can hurt, ___ loving can hurt ___ sometimes

| |B5 | |Asus2 |
But it's the on - ly thing that I ___ know.

| |E |
And when it gets hard

| |C#5 |
You know it can get hard ___ sometimes.

| |B5 | |Asus2 | |
It is the on - ly thing that makes ___ us feel alive.

Pre-Chorus 1

‖C#m |Asus2 |
We keep this love in a photo - graph,

|E |B5
We made these memories for ourselves.

|C#m |Asus2
Where our eyes are never closing, hearts are never broken,

|E |
And time's forever frozen still.

Chorus 1

|Bsus4 ‖E |
So you can keep me

| |B5 |
Inside the pocket of your ripped jeans,

| |C#m |
Holding me closer till our eyes meet,

| |Asus2 |
You won't ever be alone.

| |E |
Wait for me to come home.

Verse 2

```
                    |  N.C.              ‖E       |                    |C♯5           |
                    Loving can heal, ___      loving can mend ___ your soul
                    |                   |B5        |                   |Asus2        |
                    And it's the on - ly thing that I ___ know, know.
                    |                         |E
                    I swear it will get eas - ier,
                    |                                    |C♯5
                    Re - member that with every piece ___ of you.
                        |              |B5
                    Mm, ___ and it's the on - ly thing
                        |                        |Asus2       |            |
                    We take with us when we die.              Mm.
```

Pre-Chorus 2

```
                    ‖C♯m                    |Asus2     |
                        We keep this love in a photo - graph,
                    |E                          |B5
                        We made these memories for ourselves.
                           |C♯m               |Asus2
                    Where our eyes were never closing, hearts were never broken,
                        |E
                    And time's forever frozen still.
```

Chorus 2

```
                    |Bsus4         ‖E        |
                        So you can keep me
                    |                        |B5           |
                    Inside the pocket of your ripped jeans,
                    |                        |C♯m          |
                    Holding me closer till our eyes meet,
                    |                        |Asus2        |
                    You won't ever be alone.
                    |                 |E            |
                        And if you hurt me, well, that's O.K. baby,
                    |B5            |                    |C♯5          |
                    Only words bleed inside these pages you just hold me,
                    |                 |Asus2       |
                    I won't ever let you go.
```

Bridge

```
|                                    ‖ C#5        |
Wait for me to come home.
|                                    | Asus2       |
Wait for me to come home.
|                                    | E           |
Wait for me to come home.
|                                    | Bsus4       |
Wait for me to come home, ___ ooh.
```

Chorus 3

```
|                          ‖ E            |
        Oh, you can fit me
        |                                     | Bsus4      |
Inside the necklace you got when you were sixteen,
|                                | C#m        |
Next to your heartbeat, where I should be,
|                            | Asus2      |
Keep it deep within your soul.
|              | E          |
        And if you hurt me, well, that's O.K. baby,
        | Bsus4         |                        | C#m     |
Only words bleed inside these pages, you just hold me,
|                       | Asus2      |
I won't ever let you go.
```

Outro

```
|                              ‖ E          |
        And when I'm away
|                                  | Bsus4      |
I will remember how you kissed me
|                                 | C#m        |
Under the lamp post back on 6th Street
|                                    | Asus2      |
Hearing you whisper through the phone.
|     N.C.                        ‖
Wait for me to come home.
```

Sing

Words and Music by
Ed Sheeran and Pharrell Williams

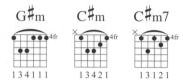

G#m   C#m   C#m7

Intro   ‖ G#m | | |

Verse 1
              | ‖ G#m |
              It's late in the eve - nin', glass on the side.
              | | |
              I've been sat with you ___ for most of the night.
              | | C#m |
              Ignorin' ev'rybody here, we wish they would disappear
                        | | |
So maybe we could get down, now.
| G#m | |
  I don't wanna know ___ if you're gettin' ahead of the pro - gram.
                        | | C#m |
I want you to be mine, ___ lady, to hold your body close.
              | |
              Take another step into the no ___ man's land,
                        |
Uh, for the longest time, ___ lady.

Chorus 1
‖ G#m |
I need you, darling. Come on set the tone.
        | |
If you feel you're fallin', won't you let me know?
        | C#m7 | | | |
Ho, oo,   oh, oh, oo.
| C#m7 |
  If you love me, come on, get involved.
        | |
Feel it rushin' through you from your head to toe.
        | C#m7 | | | |
Oh, ___   oh, oh, oo.   *Sing!*

Imterlude 1

‖ **G♯m** | | | |
(Oh, _____ oh.) _____ *Louder!*
| **C♯m** | | |
(Oh,) _____ *sing!* (oh.)

Verse 2

| ‖ **G♯m**
This love is ablaze. ____ I saw flames from the side of the stage

|
And the fire ____ brigade comes in a couple of days.

|
Until then, we got nothin' to say and nothin' to know

| |
But somethin' to drink and maybe somethin' to smoke.
| **C♯m**
Let it go until our roads are changed,

| |
Singing, we found love in a local rave, no.

|
I don't really know what I'm supposed to say,

| |
But I can just figure it out and hope and pray.
| **G♯m**
I told her my name. I said, "It's nice to meet you."

| |
Then she handed me a bottle of water with tequila.

|
I already know it, she's a keeper

|
Just from this one small act of kindness.
| **C♯m**
I'm in   deep. If anybody finds out,

|
I meant ____ to drive home but I drank all of it, now.

|
Not   sobering up, we just sit on the couch.

|
One thing ____ led to another, now she's kissin' my mouth.

Chorus 2   *Repeat Chorus 1*

Interlude 2   *Repeat Interlude 1*

Bridge

     ‖**G♯m** |

(Can you feel ____ it?) All the guys in here don't even wanna dance.

                   | |

(Can you feel ____ it?) All that I can hear is music from the back.

           |**C♯m7**

(Can you feel ____ it?) Found you hidin' here,

     | | |

So won't you take my hand, darlin',   before the beat kicks in a - gain?

         |**G♯m7** | | |

(Can you feel ____ it?)   Oo, above.

| |**C♯m7** | |

   Can you feel ____ it?   Oh, Lord, oh, ____ no,

        |

Whoa, ____ oh, lo, lo. *Sing!*

Outro-Chorus

    ‖**G♯m** |

I need you, darlin', come on set the tone.

        | |

If you feel you're fallin', won't you let me know?

  |**C♯m7** | | | |

Ho, oo,   oh, oh, oo.   *Sing!*

|**G♯m7** |

 If you love me, come on, get involved.

        | |

Feel it rushin' through you from your head to toe.

  |**C♯m7** | | | **N.C.**   ‖

Oh, oo,   oh, oh, oo.   *Sing!*

Small Bump

Words and Music by
Ed Sheeran

(Capo 3rd fret)

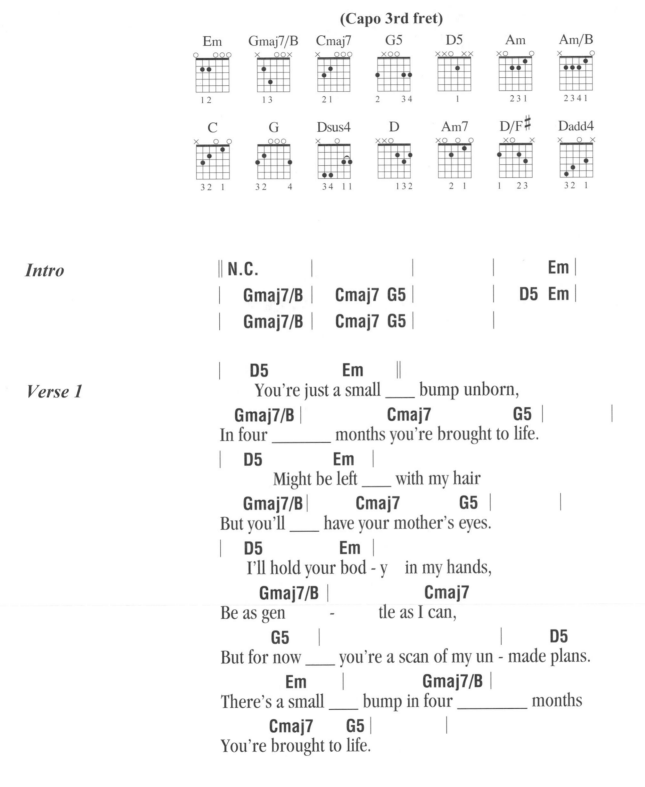

Intro

	N.C.			Em
Gmaj7/B	Cmaj7 G5		D5 Em
Gmaj7/B	Cmaj7 G5	

Verse 1

| D5 Em ||
You're just a small ___ bump unborn,
Gmaj7/B | Cmaj7 G5 | |
In four _____ months you're brought to life.
| D5 Em |
Might be left ___ with my hair
Gmaj7/B | Cmaj7 G5 | |
But you'll ___ have your mother's eyes.
| D5 Em |
I'll hold your bod - y in my hands,
Gmaj7/B | Cmaj7
Be as gen - tle as I can,
G5 | | D5
But for now ___ you're a scan of my un - made plans.
Em | Gmaj7/B |
There's a small ___ bump in four _____ months
Cmaj7 G5 | |
You're brought to life.

Pre-Chorus 1

```
                              Am ‖          Am/B |
           And I'll whisper ____ quietly
|                   C                 G        |
           And give you nothing but truth.
|                         Am|             Am/B|
           If you're not in  -  side me,
|              C            Dsus4 |            |
           I'll put my future in you.
```

Chorus 1

```
|               Em     ‖   Gmaj7/B |    Cmaj7   G5|
           You are my one ____ and on   -       ly
|                         |                Em      |
           And you can wrap your fingers 'round my thumb
|        Gmaj7/B |   Cmaj7   G5   |            |
           And hold _____ me       tight.
|   D5            Em    |   Gmaj7/B |    Cmaj7   G5 |
           Oh, you are my one ____ and on   -     ly
|                         |                Em      |
           You can wrap your fingers 'round my thumb
|        Gmaj7/B |   Cmaj7   G5   |
           And hold _____ me       tight.
|                |
           And you will be all right.
```

Verse 2

```
           |                 ‖ G5
   Ooh, ____ you're just a small bump I know,
   Gmaj7/B |           Cmaj7   G5   |        |
   You'll _____ grow into your skin.
   |   D5          Em     |
           With a smile ____ like hers
       Gmaj7/B |   Cmaj7        G5  |         |
   And a dim    -     ple beneath your chin.
   |   D5     Em  |                 Gmaj7/B |        Cmaj7
           Fin  -  gernails the size of a half _____ grain of rice
   G5   |                        |    D5
   And eye  -  lids closed to be soon ____ open wide.
    Em      |           Gmaj7/B |
   A small _____ bump in four _____ months
   Cmaj7         G5   |        |
   You'll open your eyes.
```

46

Pre-Chorus 2

```
                          |        Am ‖       Am/B |
                          And I'll hold you ____ tightly
                          |      C        G      |            |
                          And tell you nothing but truth
                          |              Am |       Am/B |
                          If you're not in  -  side me,
                          |       C        Dsus4 |        |
                          I'll put my future in you.
```

Chorus 2

Repeat Chorus 1

Bridge

```
              D ‖           Am7 |                    Em    |
              Then you can lie     with me, with your tin  -  y feet.
                          G  |                 D  |
              When you're half-asleep I'll leave you be,
              |        Am7 |        Em    |
              Right in front   of me for a coup - le weeks
D/F♯  G  |                       |C   Dadd4 |         |
So     I    could keep you safe.
```

Chorus 3

```
              |                Em ‖      Gmaj7/B |   Cmaj7   G5 |
              'Cause you are my one ____ and on  -  ly
              |              |               Em    |
              And you can wrap your fingers 'round my thumb
              |    Gmaj7/B |   Cmaj7   G5 |        |
              And hold _____ me      tight.
              | Am7      Em   |   Gmaj7/B |    Cmaj7      G5 |
              You are my one ____ and on  -  ly
              |              |               Em    |
              You can wrap your fingers 'round my thumb
              |    Gmaj7/B |   Cmaj7   G5 |
              And hold _____ me      tight.
              |              |          |
              And you will be all right.
```

Outro

```
              |                          ‖ Em
              'Cause you were just a small ____ bump unborn,
              Gmaj7/B |       Cmaj7        G   |        |
              For four _____ months then torn from life.
              |                   | Em
              Maybe you were need - ed up there
              Gmaj7/B |    Cmaj7   | G5      ‖
              But we're ____ still  unaware as why.
```

Thinking Out Loud

Words and Music by
Ed Sheeran and Amy Wadge

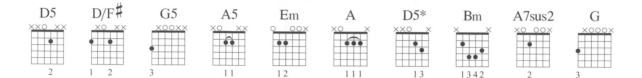

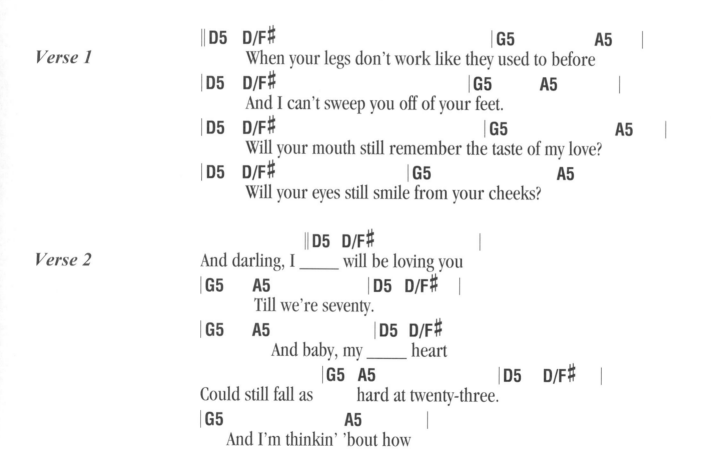

Verse 1

‖D5 D/F♯ |G5   A5 |
When your legs don't work like they used to before

|D5 D/F♯ |G5   A5 |
And I can't sweep you off of your feet.

|D5 D/F♯ |G5   A5 |
Will your mouth still remember the taste of my love?

|D5 D/F♯ |G5   A5
Will your eyes still smile from your cheeks?

Verse 2

                ‖D5 D/F♯ |
And darling, I ____ will be loving you

|G5   A5 |D5 D/F♯ |
Till we're seventy.

|G5   A5 |D5 D/F♯ |
And baby, my ____ heart

                    |G5 A5 |D5   D/F♯ |
Could still fall as   hard at twenty-three.

|G5   A5 |
And I'm thinkin' 'bout how

Pre-Chorus 1

```
‖Em                          |A    D*    |
  People fall in love in myster - ious ways.
|Em                          |A
 Maybe just the touch of a hand.
    |Em                      |A       Bm
Well, me, I fall in love with you ev - 'ry single day
     |Em                     |A7sus2
And I just wanna tell you I am.
```

Chorus 1

```
N.C              ‖D5  D/F♯    |
So honey, now.
|G5       A5                   |D5     D/F♯  |
  Take me into your loving arms.
|G5       A5                   |D5      D/F♯   |
  Kiss ___ me under the light of a thousand stars.
|G5       A5                        |D5    D/F♯
  Place ___ your head on my beating heart.
           |G   A
I'm thinking out loud.
     |Bm  A    G   D/F♯   |
Maybe we   found love right
|Em    A   D5        |
 Where we are.
```

Verse 3

```
‖D5   D/F♯                          |G5           A5      |
     When my hair's all but gone and my memory fades
|D5   D/F♯                          |G5   A5      |
     And the crowds don't remember my name.
|D5   D/F♯                |G5           A5            |
     When my hands don't play the strings the same way.
|D5   D/F♯                    |G5    A5
     I know you will still love me the same.
```

Verse 4

```
                        ‖D5  D/F#
'Cause, honey, your ____ soul
                      |G5   A5              |D5  D/F#  |
Could never grow        old, it's evergreen.
|G5   A5              |D5  D/F#
      And baby your ___ smile's
                    |G5    A5              |D5    D/F#  |
Forever in ___  my mind and memory.
|G5              A5           |
      I'm thinkin' 'bout how…
```

Pre-Chorus 2

```
‖Em                   |A     D*
  People fall in love in myster - ious ways
   |Em                        |A
And maybe it's all part of a plan.
      |Em                          |A      Bm       |
Well, I'll just keep on making the same ___ mis - takes
|Em                        |A7sus2
  Hoping that you'll understand.
```

Chorus 2

```
N.C.                   ‖D5  D/F#   |
      That baby, now.
|G5      A5                |D5     D/F#   |
      Take me into your loving arms.
|G5      A5                      |D5      D/F#  |
      Kiss ___ me under the light of a thousand stars.
|G5      A5                          |D5   D/F#
      Place ___ your head on my beating heart.
                      |G    A
I'm thinking out ___  loud.
             |Bm  A    G   D/F#   |
And maybe we  found love right
|Em    A  D5           |
 Where we are, oh, oh.
```

Guitar Solo ‖D   D/F# |G   A |D   D/F# |G   A |

|D   D/F# |G   A |D   D/F# |

|G   A   ‖D5 D/F# |

Chorus 3 So baby, now

|G5   A5 |D5   D/F# |

Take me into your loving arms.

|G5   A5   D5   D/F#

Kiss ___ me under the light of a thousand stars.

    |G5   A5 |D5   D/F#

Oh, dar - lin', place ___ your head on my beating heart.

     |G A

I'm thinking out ___ loud.

    |Bm A   G   D/F# |

That maybe we found love right

|Em   A D5

 Where we are.

    |Bm A   G   D/F# |

And baby, we found love right

|Em   A D5

 Where we are.

    |Bm A   G   D/F# |

And we found love right

|Em   A D5   ‖

 Where we are.

STRUM & SING

Lyrics, chord symbols, and guitar chord diagrams for your favorite songs.

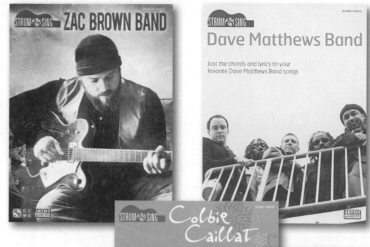

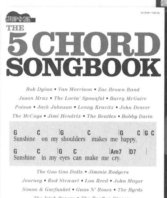

GUITAR

SARA BAREILLES
00102354...............................$12.99

ZAC BROWN BAND
02501620...............................$12.99

COLBIE CAILLAT
02501725...............................$14.99

CAMPFIRE FOLK SONGS
02500686...............................$10.99

CHART HITS OF 2014-2015
00142554...............................$12.99

BEST OF KENNY CHESNEY
00142457...............................$14.99

JOHN DENVER COLLECTION
02500632...............................$9.95

EASY ACOUSTIC SONGS
00125478...............................$12.99

50 CHILDREN'S SONGS
02500825...............................$7.95

THE 5 CHORD SONGBOOK
02501718...............................$10.99

FOLK SONGS
02501482...............................$9.99

FOLK/ROCK FAVORITES
02501669...............................$9.99

40 POP/ROCK HITS
02500633...............................$9.95

THE 4 CHORD SONGBOOK
02501533...............................$10.99

THE 4-CHORD COUNTRY SONGBOOK
00114936...............................$12.99

HITS OF THE '60S
02501138...............................$10.95

HITS OF THE '70S
02500871...............................$9.99

HYMNS
02501125...............................$8.99

JACK JOHNSON
02500858...............................$16.99

CAROLE KING
00115243...............................$10.99

DAVE MATTHEWS BAND
02501078...............................$10.95

JOHN MAYER
02501636...............................$10.99

INGRID MICHAELSON
02501634...............................$10.99

THE MOST REQUESTED SONGS
02501748...............................$10.99

JASON MRAZ
02501452...............................$14.99

PRAISE & WORSHIP
00152381...............................$12.99

ROCK AROUND THE CLOCK
00103625...............................$12.99

ROCK BALLADS
02500872...............................$9.95

ED SHEERAN
00152016...............................$12.99

THE 6 CHORD SONGBOOK
02502277...............................$10.99

CAT STEVENS
00116827...............................$10.99

TODAY'S HITS
00119301...............................$10.99

KEITH URBAN
00118558...............................$12.99

NEIL YOUNG – GREATEST HITS
00138270...............................$12.99

UKULELE

COLBIE CAILLAT
02501731...............................$10.99

JOHN DENVER
02501694...............................$10.99

JACK JOHNSON
02501702...............................$15.99

JOHN MAYER
02501706...............................$10.99

INGRID MICHAELSON
02501741...............................$10.99

THE MOST REQUESTED SONGS
02501453...............................$14.99

JASON MRAZ
02501753...............................$14.99

SING-ALONG SONGS
02501710...............................$14.99

HAL•LEONARD® CORPORATION

7777 W. Bluemound Rd. P.O. Box 13819 Milwaukee, WI 53213

Prices, content, and availability subject to change without notice.

Guitar Chord Songbooks

Each 6" x 9" book includes complete lyrics, chord symbols, and guitar chord diagrams.

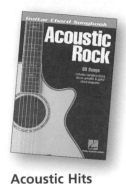
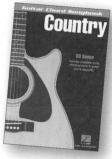
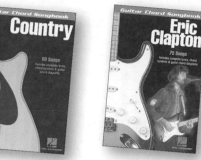
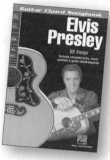

Acoustic Hits
00701787 . . . . $14.99
Acoustic Rock
00699540 . . . . $17.95
Adele
00102761 . . . . $14.99
Alabama
00699914 . . . . $14.95
The Beach Boys
00699566 . . . . $14.95
The Beatles (A-I)
00699558 . . . . $17.99
The Beatles (J-Y)
00699562 . . . . $17.99
Bluegrass
00702585 . . . . $14.99
Blues
00699733 . . . . $12.95
Broadway
00699920 . . . . $14.99
Johnny Cash
00699648 . . . . $17.99
Steven Curtis Chapman
00700702 . . . . $17.99
Children's Songs
00699539 . . . . $16.99
Christmas Carols
00699536 . . . . $12.99
Christmas Songs – 2nd Edition
00119911 . . . . $14.99
Eric Clapton
00699567 . . . . $15.99
Classic Rock
00699598 . . . . $15.99
Coffeehouse Hits
00703318 . . . . $14.99
Country
00699534 . . . . $14.99
Country Favorites
00700609 . . . . $14.99
Country Hits
00140859 . . . . $14.99
Country Standards
00700608 . . . . $12.95
Cowboy Songs
00699636 . . . . $12.95
Creedence Clearwater Revival
00701786 . . . . $12.99
Crosby, Stills & Nash
00701609 . . . . $12.99
John Denver
02501697 . . . . $14.99
Neil Diamond
00700606 . . . . $14.99

Disney
00701071 . . . . $14.99
The Best of Bob Dylan
14037617 . . . . $17.99
Eagles
00122917 . . . . $16.99
Early Rock
00699916 . . . . $14.99
Folksongs
00699541 . . . . $12.95
Folk Pop Rock
00699651 . . . . $14.95
40 Easy Strumming Songs
00115972 . . . . $14.99
Four Chord Songs
00701611 . . . . $12.99
Glee
00702501 . . . . $14.99
Gospel Hymns
00700463 . . . . $14.99
Grand Ole Opry®
00699885 . . . . $16.95
Green Day
00103074 . . . . $12.99
Guitar Chord Songbook White Pages
00702609 . . . . $29.99
Irish Songs
00701044 . . . . $14.99
Billy Joel
00699632 . . . . $15.99
Elton John
00699732 . . . . $15.99
Ray LaMontagne
00130337 . . . . $12.99
Latin Songs
00700973 . . . . $14.99
Love Songs
00701043 . . . . $14.99
Bob Marley
00701704 . . . . $12.99
Bruno Mars
00125332 . . . . $12.99
Paul McCartney
00385035 . . . . $16.95
Steve Miller
00701146 . . . . $12.99

Modern Worship
00701801 . . . . $16.99
Motown
00699734 . . . . $16.95
The 1950s
00699922 . . . . $14.99
The 1980s
00700551 . . . . $16.99
Nirvana
00699762 . . . . $16.99
Roy Orbison
00699752 . . . . $12.95
Peter, Paul & Mary
00103013 . . . . $12.99
Tom Petty
00699883 . . . . $15.99
Pop/Rock
00699538 . . . . $14.95
Praise & Worship
00699634 . . . . $14.99
Elvis Presley
00699633 . . . . $14.95
Queen
00702395 . . . . $12.99
Rascal Flatts
00130951 . . . . $12.99
Red Hot Chili Peppers
00699710 . . . . $16.95
Rock Ballads
00701034 . . . . $14.99
Rock 'n' Roll
00699535 . . . . $14.95
Bob Seger
00701147 . . . . $12.99
Carly Simon
00121011 . . . . $14.99
Singer/Songwriter Songs
00126053 . . . . $14.99
Sting
00699921 . . . . $14.99
Taylor Swift
00701799 . . . . $15.99
Three Chord Acoustic Songs
00123860 . . . . $14.99
Three Chord Songs
00699720 . . . . $12.95
Today's Hits
00120983 . . . . $14.99
Top 100 Hymns Guitar Songbook
75718017 . . . . $14.99
Two-Chord Songs
00119236 . . . . $14.99
Ultimate-Guitar
00702617 . . . . $24.99
U2
00137744 . . . . $14.99
Wedding Songs
00701005 . . . . $14.99
Hank Williams
00700607 . . . . $14.99
Stevie Wonder
00120862 . . . . $14.99
Neil Young–Decade
00700464 . . . . $14.99

Prices, contents, and availability subject to change without notice.

HAL•LEONARD®
CORPORATION

7777 W. BLUEMOUND RD. P.O. BOX 13819 MILWAUKEE, WI 53213

Visit Hal Leonard online at **www.halleonard.com**

0915

HAL LEONARD GUITAR CHEAT SHEETS

The Hal Leonard Cheat Sheets series includes lyrics, chord frames, and "rhythm tab" (cut-to-the-chase notation) to make playing easier than ever! No music reading is required, and all the songs are presented on two-page spreads to avoid page turns.

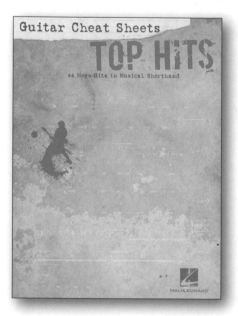

TOP HITS

44 pop favorites, including: Are You Gonna Be My Girl • Baby • Bad Day • Bubbly • Clocks • Crazy • Fireflies • Gives You Hell • Hey, Soul Sister • How to Save a Life • I Gotta Feeling • Just the Way You Are • Lucky • Mercy • Mr. Brightside • Need You Now • Take Me Out • Toes • Use Somebody • Viva La Vida • You Belong with Me • and more.
00701646 ....$14.99

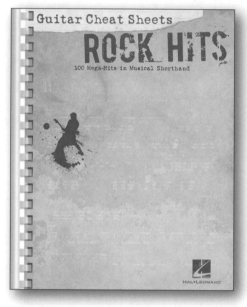

ROCK HITS

44 songs, including: Are You Gonna Go My Way • Black Hole Sun • Counting Blue Cars • Float On • Friday I'm in Love • Gives You Hell • Grenade • Jeremy • Kryptonite • Push • Scar Tissue • Semi-Charmed Life • Smells like Teen Spirit • Smooth • Thnks Fr Th Mmrs • Two Princes • Use Somebody • Viva La Vida • Where Is the Love • You Oughta Know • and more.
00702392 ....$24.99

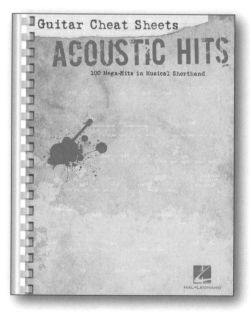

ACOUSTIC HITS

100 unplugged megahits in musical shorthand: All Apologies • Crazy Little Thing Called Love • Creep • Daughter • Every Rose Has Its Thorn • Hallelujah • I'm Yours • The Lazy Song • Little Lion Man • Love Story • More Than Words • Patience • Strong Enough • 21 Guns • Wanted Dead or Alive • Wonderwall • and more.
00702391 ....$24.99

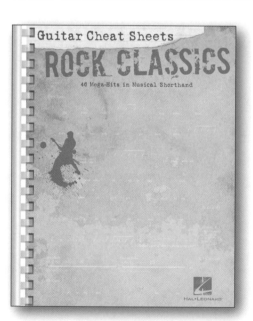

ROCK CLASSICS

Nearly 50 classics, including: All Right Now • Barracuda • Born to Be Wild • Carry on Wayward Son • Cat Scratch Fever • Free Ride • Layla • Message in a Bottle • Paranoid • Proud Mary • Rhiannon • Rock and Roll All Nite • Slow Ride • Smoke on the Water • Sweet Home Alabama • Welcome to the Jungle • You Shook Me All Night Long • and more.
00702393 ....$24.99

HAL•LEONARD® CORPORATION

7777 W. BLUEMOUND RD. P.O. BOX 13819 MILWAUKEE, WI 53213

Visit Hal Leonard online at **www.halleonard.com**

Prices, contents, and availability subject to change without notice.   0712

easy GUITAR play along

Audio Access Included

INCLUDES TAB

The *Easy Guitar Play Along*® Series features streamlined transcriptions of your favorite songs. Just follow the tab, listen to the audio to hear how the guitar should sound, and then play along using the backing tracks. The CD is playable on any CD player, and is also enhanced to include the Amazing Slowdowner technology so Mac and PC users can adjust the recording to any tempo without changing the pitch!

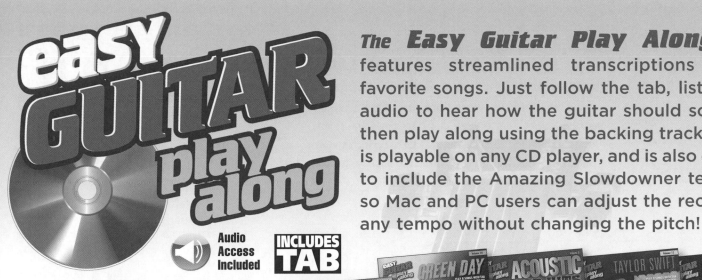

1. ROCK CLASSICS

Jailbreak • Living After Midnight • Mississippi Queen • Rocks Off • Runnin' Down a Dream • Smoke on the Water • Strutter • Up Around the Bend.

00702560 Book/CD Pack....... $14.99

2. ACOUSTIC TOP HITS

About a Girl • I'm Yours • The Lazy Song • The Scientist • 21 Guns • Upside Down • What I Got • Wonderwall.

00702569 Book/CD Pack....... $14.99

3. ROCK HITS

All the Small Things • Best of You • Brain Stew (The Godzilla Remix) • Californication • Island in the Sun • Plush • Smells like Teen Spirit • Use Somebody.

00702570 Book/CD Pack....... $14.99

4. ROCK 'N' ROLL

Blue Suede Shoes • I Get Around • I'm a Believer • Jailhouse Rock • Oh, Pretty Woman • Peggy Sue • Runaway • Wake up Little Susie.

00702572 Book/CD Pack..... $14.99

5. ULTIMATE ACOUSTIC

Against the Wind • Babe, I'm Gonna Leave You • Come Monday • Free Fallin' • Give a Little Bit • Have You Ever Seen the Rain? • New Kid in Town • We Can Work It Out.

00702573 Book/CD Pack........ $14.99

6. CHRISTMAS SONGS

Have Yourself a Merry Little Christmas • A Holly Jolly Christmas • The Little Drummer Boy • Run Rudolph Run • Santa Claus Is Comin' to Town • Silver and Gold • Sleigh Ride • Winter Wonderland.

00101879 Book/CD Pack......... $14.99

7. BLUES SONGS FOR BEGINNERS

Come On (Part 1) • Double Trouble • Gangster of Love • I'm Ready • Let Me Love You Baby • Mary Had a Little Lamb • San-Ho-Zay • T-Bone Shuffle.

00103235 Book/CD Pack.....$14.99

8. ACOUSTIC SONGS FOR BEGINNERS

Barely Breathing • Drive • Everlong • Good Riddance (Time of Your Life) • Hallelujah • Hey There Delilah • Lake of Fire • Photograph.

00103240 Book/CD Pack.....$14.99

9. ROCK SONGS FOR BEGINNERS

Are You Gonna Be My Girl • Buddy Holly • Everybody Hurts • In Bloom • Otherside • The Rock Show • Santa Monica • When I Come Around.

00103255 Book/CD Pack.....$14.99

10. GREEN DAY

Basket Case • Boulevard of Broken Dreams • Good Riddance (Time of Your Life) • Holiday • Longview • 21 Guns • Wake Me up When September Ends • When I Come Around.

00122322 Book/CD Pack.....$14.99

11. NIRVANA

All Apologies • Come As You Are • Heart Shaped Box • Lake of Fire • Lithium • The Man Who Sold the World • Rape Me • Smells like Teen Spirit.

00122325 Book/CD Pack.....$14.99

12. TAYLOR SWIFT

Fifteen • Love Story • Mean • Picture to Burn • Red • We Are Never Ever Getting Back Together • White Horse • You Belong with Me.

00122326 Book/CD Pack.....$16.99

14. JIMI HENDRIX – SMASH HITS

All Along the Watchtower • Can You See Me • Crosstown Traffic • Fire • Foxey Lady • Hey Joe • Manic Depression • Purple Haze • Red House • Remember • Stone Free • The Wind Cries Mary.

00130591 Book/ Online Audio........ $24.99

HAL•LEONARD® CORPORATION

7777 W. BLUEMOUND RD. P.O. BOX 13819 MILWAUKEE, WI 53213

www.halleonard.com

Prices, contents, and availability subject to change without notice.

This series will help you play your favorite songs quickly and easily. Just follow the tab and listen to the audio to the hear how the guitar should sound, and then play along using the separate backing tracks. Mac or PC users can also slow down the tempo without changing pitch by using the CD in their computer. The melody and lyrics are included in the book so that you can sing or simply follow along.

INCLUDES TAB

VOL. 1 – ROCK	00699570 / $16.99
VOL. 2 – ACOUSTIC	00699569 / $16.95
VOL. 3 – HARD ROCK	00699573 / $16.95
VOL. 4 – POP/ROCK	00699571 / $16.99
VOL. 5 – MODERN ROCK	00699574 / $16.99
VOL. 6 – '90S ROCK	00699572 / $16.99
VOL. 7 – BLUES	00699575 / $16.95
VOL. 8 – ROCK	00699585 / $14.99
VOL. 10 – ACOUSTIC	00699586 / $16.95
VOL. 11 – EARLY ROCK	00699579 / $14.95
VOL. 12 – POP/ROCK	00699587 / $14.95
VOL. 13 – FOLK ROCK	00699581 / $15.99
VOL. 14 – BLUES ROCK	00699582 / $16.95
VOL. 15 – R&B	00699583 / $14.95
VOL. 16 – JAZZ	00699584 / $15.95
VOL. 17 – COUNTRY	00699588 / $15.95
VOL. 18 – ACOUSTIC ROCK	00699577 / $15.95
VOL. 19 – SOUL	00699578 / $14.99
VOL. 20 – ROCKABILLY	00699580 / $14.95
VOL. 21 – YULETIDE	00699602 / $14.95
VOL. 22 – CHRISTMAS	00699600 / $15.95
VOL. 23 – SURF	00699635 / $14.95
VOL. 24 – ERIC CLAPTON	00699649 / $17.99
VOL. 25 – LENNON & MCCARTNEY	00699642 / $16.99
VOL. 26 – ELVIS PRESLEY	00699643 / $14.95
VOL. 27 – DAVID LEE ROTH	00699645 / $16.95
VOL. 28 – GREG KOCH	00699646 / $14.95
VOL. 29 – BOB SEGER	00699647 / $15.99
VOL. 30 – KISS	00699644 / $16.99
VOL. 31 – CHRISTMAS HITS	00699652 / $14.95
VOL. 32 – THE OFFSPRING	00699653 / $14.95
VOL. 33 – ACOUSTIC CLASSICS	00699656 / $16.95
VOL. 34 – CLASSIC ROCK	00699658 / $16.95
VOL. 35 – HAIR METAL	00699660 / $16.95
VOL. 36 – SOUTHERN ROCK	00699661 / $16.95
VOL. 37 – ACOUSTIC UNPLUGGED	00699662 / $22.99
VOL. 38 – BLUES	00699663 / $16.95
VOL. 39 – '80S METAL	00699664 / $16.99
VOL. 40 – INCUBUS	00699668 / $17.95
VOL. 41 – ERIC CLAPTON	00699669 / $16.95
VOL. 42 – 2000S ROCK	00699670 / $16.99
VOL. 43 – LYNYRD SKYNYRD	00699681 / $17.95
VOL. 44 – JAZZ	00699689 / $14.99
VOL. 45 – TV THEMES	00699718 / $14.95
VOL. 46 – MAINSTREAM ROCK	00699722 / $16.95
VOL. 47 – HENDRIX SMASH HITS	00699723 / $19.95
VOL. 48 – AEROSMITH CLASSICS	00699724 / $17.99
VOL. 49 – STEVIE RAY VAUGHAN	00699725 / $17.99
VOL. 50 – VAN HALEN 1978-1984	00110269 / $17.99
VOL. 51 – ALTERNATIVE '90S	00699727 / $14.99
VOL. 52 – FUNK	00699728 / $14.95
VOL. 53 – DISCO	00699729 / $14.99
VOL. 54 – HEAVY METAL	00699730 / $14.95
VOL. 55 – POP METAL	00699731 / $14.95
VOL. 56 – FOO FIGHTERS	00699749 / $15.99
VOL. 57 – SYSTEM OF A DOWN	00699751 / $14.95
VOL. 58 – BLINK-182	00699772 / $14.95
VOL. 59 – CHET ATKINS	00702347 / $16.99
VOL. 60 – 3 DOORS DOWN	00699774 / $14.95
VOL. 61 – SLIPKNOT	00699775 / $16.99
VOL. 62 – CHRISTMAS CAROLS	00699798 / $12.95

VOL. 63 – CREEDENCE CLEARWATER REVIVAL	00699802 / $16.99
VOL. 64 – THE ULTIMATE OZZY OSBOURNE	00699803 / $16.99
VOL. 66 – THE ROLLING STONES	00699807 / $16.95
VOL. 67 – BLACK SABBATH	00699808 / $16.99
VOL. 68 – PINK FLOYD – DARK SIDE OF THE MOON	00699809 / $16.99
VOL. 69 – ACOUSTIC FAVORITES	00699810 / $14.95
VOL. 70 – OZZY OSBOURNE	00699805 / $16.99
VOL. 71 – CHRISTIAN ROCK	00699824 / $14.95
VOL. 73 – BLUESY ROCK	00699829 / $16.99
VOL. 75 – TOM PETTY	00699882 / $16.99
VOL. 76 – COUNTRY HITS	00699884 / $14.95
VOL. 77 – BLUEGRASS	00699910 / $14.99
VOL. 78 – NIRVANA	00700132 / $16.99
VOL. 79 – NEIL YOUNG	00700133 / $24.99
VOL. 80 – ACOUSTIC ANTHOLOGY	00700175 / $19.95
VOL. 81 – ROCK ANTHOLOGY	00700176 / $22.99
VOL. 82 – EASY SONGS	00700177 / $12.99
VOL. 83 – THREE CHORD SONGS	00700178 / $16.99
VOL. 84 – STEELY DAN	00700200 / $16.99
VOL. 85 – THE POLICE	00700269 / $16.99
VOL. 86 – BOSTON	00700465 / $16.99
VOL. 87 – ACOUSTIC WOMEN	00700763 / $14.99
VOL. 88 – GRUNGE	00700467 / $16.99
VOL. 89 – REGGAE	00700468 / $15.99
VOL. 90 – CLASSICAL POP	00700469 / $14.99
VOL. 91 – BLUES INSTRUMENTALS	00700505 / $14.99
VOL. 92 – EARLY ROCK INSTRUMENTALS	00700506 / $14.99
VOL. 93 – ROCK INSTRUMENTALS	00700507 / $16.99
VOL. 94 – SLOW BLUES	00700508 / $16.99
VOL. 95 – BLUES CLASSICS	00700509 / $14.99
VOL. 96 – THIRD DAY	00700560 / $14.95
VOL. 97 – ROCK BAND	00700703 / $14.99
VOL. 99 – ZZ TOP	00700762 / $16.99
VOL. 100 – B.B. KING	00700466 / $16.99
VOL. 101 – SONGS FOR BEGINNERS	00701917 / $14.99
VOL. 102 – CLASSIC PUNK	00700769 / $14.99
VOL. 103 – SWITCHFOOT	00700773 / $16.99
VOL. 104 – DUANE ALLMAN	00700846 / $16.99
VOL. 105 – LATIN	00700939 / $16.99
VOL. 106 – WEEZER	00700958 / $14.99
VOL. 107 – CREAM	00701069 / $16.99
VOL. 108 – THE WHO	00701053 / $16.99
VOL. 109 – STEVE MILLER	00701054 / $14.99
VOL. 110 – SLIDE GUITAR HITS	00701055 / $16.99
VOL. 111 – JOHN MELLENCAMP	00701056 / $14.99
VOL. 112 – QUEEN	00701052 / $16.99
VOL. 113 – JIM CROCE	00701058 / $15.99
VOL. 114 – BON JOVI	00701060 / $14.99
VOL. 115 – JOHNNY CASH	00701070 / $16.99
VOL. 116 – THE VENTURES	00701124 / $14.99
VOL. 117 – BRAD PAISLEY	00701224 / $16.99
VOL. 118 – ERIC JOHNSON	00701353 / $16.99
VOL. 119 – AC/DC CLASSICS	00701356 / $17.99
VOL. 120 – PROGRESSIVE ROCK	00701457 / $14.99
VOL. 121 – U2	00701508 / $16.99
VOL. 122 – CROSBY, STILLS & NASH	00701610 / $16.99
VOL. 123 – LENNON & MCCARTNEY ACOUSTIC	00701614 / $16.99
VOL. 125 – JEFF BECK	00701687 / $16.99

VOL. 126 – BOB MARLEY	00701701 / $16.99
VOL. 127 – 1970S ROCK	00701739 / $14.99
VOL. 128 – 1960S ROCK	00701740 / $14.99
VOL. 129 – MEGADETH	00701741 / $16.99
VOL. 131 – 1990S ROCK	00701743 / $14.99
VOL. 132 – COUNTRY ROCK	00701757 / $15.99
VOL. 133 – TAYLOR SWIFT	00701894 / $16.99
VOL. 134 – AVENGED SEVENFOLD	00701906 / $16.99
VOL. 136 – GUITAR THEMES	00701922 / $14.99
VOL. 137 – IRISH TUNES	00701966 / $15.99
VOL. 138 – BLUEGRASS CLASSICS	00701967 / $14.99
VOL. 139 – GARY MOORE	00702370 / $16.99
VOL. 140 – MORE STEVIE RAY VAUGHAN	00702396 / $17.99
VOL. 141 – ACOUSTIC HITS	00702401 / $16.99
VOL. 143 – SLASH	00702425 / $19.99
VOL. 144 – DJANGO REINHARDT	00702531 / $16.99
VOL. 145 – DEF LEPPARD	00702532 / $16.99
VOL. 146 – ROBERT JOHNSON	00702533 / $16.99
VOL. 147 – SIMON & GARFUNKEL	14041591 / $16.99
VOL. 148 – BOB DYLAN	14041592 / $16.99
VOL. 149 – AC/DC HITS	14041593 / $17.99
VOL. 150 – ZAKK WYLDE	02501717 / $16.99
VOL. 152 – JOE BONAMASSA	02501751 / $19.99
VOL. 153 – RED HOT CHILI PEPPERS	00702990 / $19.99
VOL. 155 – ERIC CLAPTON – FROM THE ALBUM UNPLUGGED	00703085 / $16.99
VOL. 156 – SLAYER	00703770 / $17.99
VOL. 157 – FLEETWOOD MAC	00101382 / $16.99
VOL. 158 – ULTIMATE CHRISTMAS	00101889 / $14.99
VOL. 159 – WES MONTGOMERY	00102593 / $19.99
VOL. 160 – T-BONE WALKER	00102641 / $16.99
VOL. 161 – THE EAGLES – ACOUSTIC	00102659 / $17.99
VOL. 162 – THE EAGLES HITS	00102667 / $17.99
VOL. 163 – PANTERA	00103036 / $17.99
VOL. 164 – VAN HALEN 1986-1995	00110270 / $17.99
VOL. 166 – MODERN BLUES	00700764 / $16.99
VOL. 168 – KISS	00113421 / $16.99
VOL. 169 – TAYLOR SWIFT	00115982 / $16.99
VOL. 170 – THREE DAYS GRACE	00117337 / $16.99
VOL. 171 – JAMES BROWN	00117420 / $16.99
VOL. 172 – THE DOOBIE BROTHERS	00119670 / $16.99
VOL. 174 – SCORPIONS	00122119 / $16.99
VOL. 175 – MICHAEL SCHENKER	00122127 / $16.99
VOL. 176 – BLUES BREAKERS WITH JOHN MAYALL & ERIC CLAPTON	00122132 / $19.99
VOL. 177 – ALBERT KING	00123271 / $16.99
VOL. 178 – JASON MRAZ	00124165 / $17.99
VOL. 179 – RAMONES	00127073 / $16.99
VOL. 180 – BRUNO MARS	00129706 / $16.99
VOL. 181 – JACK JOHNSON	00129854 / $16.99
VOL. 182 – SOUNDGARDEN	00138161 / $17.99
VOL. 184 – KENNY WAYNE SHEPHERD	00138258 / $17.99
VOL. 187 – JOHN DENVER	00140839 / $17.99

Complete song lists available online.

Prices, contents, and availability subject to change without notice.

HAL•LEONARD® CORPORATION

7777 W. BLUEMOUND RD. P.O. BOX 13819 MILWAUKEE, WI 53213

www.halleonard.com